DATE DUE				
DATE		ROOM	DATE	ROOM
FEB 3 '92		17		
FEB 25 '92		11		
MAR 16 '92		19		
APR 8 '92		15		
OV 5 92		20	12/210	2Kor
OV 13 '92		13		
DEC 50 '92		14		
MAR 5 '93				

THE APACHES

by Barbara A. McCall

Illustrated by Luciano Lazzarino

ROURKE PUBLICATIONS, INC.

VERO BEACH, FLORIDA 32964

CONTENTS

Library of Congress Cataloging-in-Publication Data

McCall, Barbara A., 1936-
  The Apaches / by Barbara A. McCall.
    p.   cm. —(Native American people)
  Includes index.
  Summary: Examines the history, traditional lifestyle, and current situation of the Apache Indians.
    1. Apache Indians—Juvenile literature. [1. Apache Indians. 2. Indians of North America.] I. Title. II. Series.
  E99.A6M414 1990   973'.04972—dc20   89-49498
  ISBN 0-86625-384-X   AC

INTRODUCTION

For thousands of years before Christopher Columbus reached the shores of America, many Native American groups inhabited all parts of the continent. As each new group of European explorers and white settlers moved across North America, they discovered different tribes of Native Americans. The Apache Indians lived in lands that are now Arizona, New Mexico, Texas, and northern Mexico.

The Apaches, like other native groups, are descendents of the people who migrated from Asia thousands of years ago. Those early peoples probably crossed a land bridge that once connected the areas that today we call Alaska and Siberia, which is part of the Soviet Union.

It was in the 1500s that Spanish explorers first crossed the lands of the Apaches. At that time, most Spanish were conquerors who searched for gold and took many natives as slaves. But most Apaches were too swift and alert to be taken captive. Century after century, Native American lands in the Southwest were invaded by the Spanish and Mexicans — white men who had no regard for the rights of the natives. It was not until 1848 that the U.S. Army began its war against the Apaches. At that time, the government of the United States was involved in a program to drive all Native Americans in the South and Southwest onto reservations where the land was poor and life was hard. Many Native Americans died because of this cruel treatment.

By 1886, the U.S. Government forced the last group of Native Americans onto a reservation. That was a group of

Apaches led by a warrior named Geronimo. The surrender of Geronimo ended the battle between the U.S. Army and the Native Americans. The government agreed to help them on reservations with money and goods. Still, too many dishonest government agents ignored the needs of the natives, using government money for themselves instead.

In 1924, all Native Americans were recognized as citizens of the United States. It was many decades before other citizens and the government of the United States began to treat them with respect and justice. Finally in the 1970s and 1980s, the government made money available to help Native Americans learn new skills, become better educated, and develop money-making businesses.

Now the American Indian is recognized as the original Native American. In Arizona and New Mexico today, more than 25,000 Apaches of different bands live on or near large reservations. There the tribal councils own and manage huge forest lands, successful ski resorts, and lumber mills. Native Americans can take pride in being able to support themselves without depending on the government.

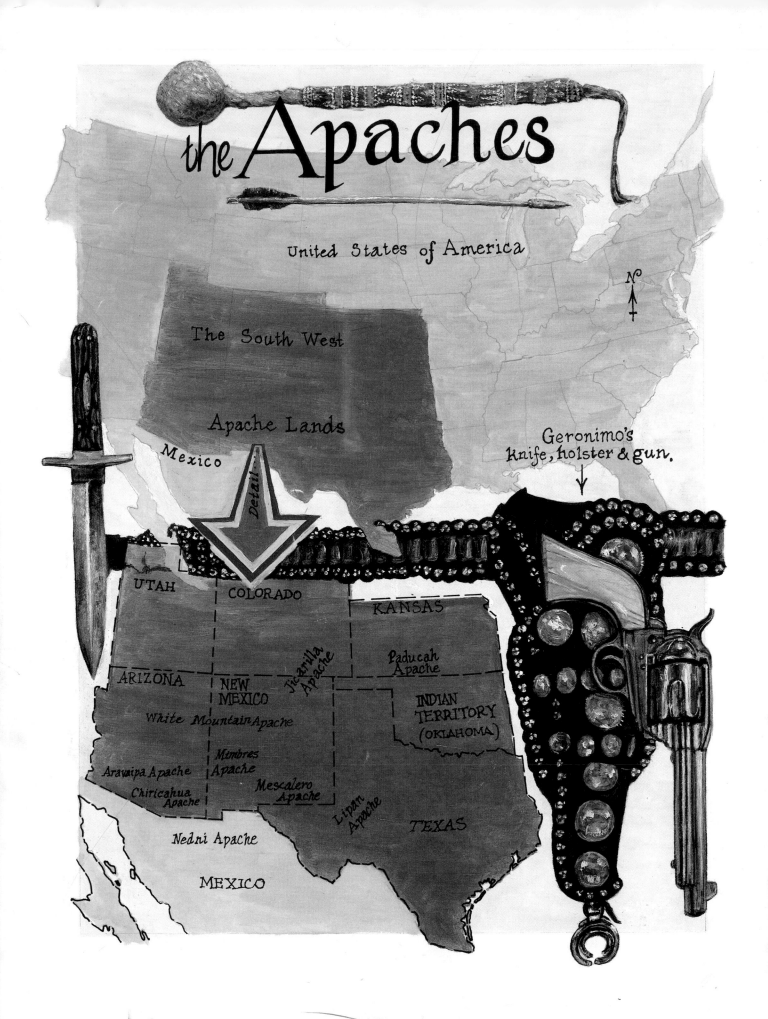

the Apaches

United States of America

N

The South West

Apache Lands

Mexico

Geronimo's
knife, holster & gun.

Detail

UTAH

COLORADO

KANSAS

Paducah
Apache

ARIZONA

NEW
MEXICO

Jicarilla
Apache

White Mountain Apache

INDIAN
TERRITORY
(OKLAHOMA)

Mimbres
Apache

Arawaipa Apache

Chiricahua
Apache

Mescalero
Apache

Lipan
Apache

TEXAS

Nedni Apache

MEXICO

Early Wanderers

The Spanish explorers and colonists were the first to come face to face with the American Indians of the Southwest. As early as 1598, the records of the Spanish colonizer of New Mexico, Don Juan de Oñate, mentioned the name Apache. The word Apache probably came from the the Zuni Indian word *apachu,* meaning "enemy." The Apaches called themselves Tin-ne-ah, which means "the people."

Apaches lived in large extended families. When a woman married, she and her husband made their home with her mother's family. An Apache husband showed respect for his mother-in-law by following her rules for the family. It was tradition that the husband always lowered his eyes in her presence.

The Apache Indians frequently raided their neighbors, the Pueblo and Zuni Indians, to settle some conflict or search for whatever they needed at the time. The Apaches often took other Indians as captives. Some captives were accepted as members of the tribe and others were made slaves.

Unlike many of their neighbors, the Apaches were a wandering group. They lived in one place for only short periods of time and then moved. They survived on plants and berries, animals of the hunt, and the spoils of war.

They were at home both on dry plains and mountains. The often lived outdoors and slept under the stars or in the shelter of a canyon. The Apaches could survive where most others would perish.

When they set up camps, the women of the tribe built the homes that were called wickiups. The wickiup was a small, dome-shaped hut that could hold only a few people. The wickiup was not a very sturdy structure. It could be put up quickly and taken apart even more quickly. A mother and daughter working together could build a wickiup in just a few hours.

First the women would find a level spot of ground and draw a circle about eight feet across. Then they dug a small trench beside the circle. Next they placed thin poles of oak or willow trees upright in the trench to make the frame for the wickiup.

The tops of the poles were pulled together and tied with strands of yucca to form the top of the shelter. The top was about five or six feet high in the center. In cold weather, an opening was left at the top of the hut so smoke could escape from the fires that were built inside. The outside of the wickiup was covered with bundles of grass and branches from trees.

The wickiup remained the traditional home of Apaches for hundreds of years. Many continued to live in them on the reservations into the early 1900s.

The Quiet Hunters

The Apache men spent most of their time hunting deer, antelope, elk, and, occasionally, buffalo. Before the 1700s, the Indians hunted on foot because they did not have horses. It was the Spanish explorers and colonists who introduced the horse to the Southwest.

In stalking a deer or antelope, a hunter might wear an animal mask made from a piece of buckskin and antlers. Wearing such masks, one or two hunters crawled quietly into an area where the animals were grazing. Sometimes hunters crawled so quietly that they got within ten feet of the animals.

Once deer were in close range, the hunter often watched the movements of the animals for a long time. Sometimes the Apache would wait in tall grass for hours until the deer came close enough for a good shot. When the time was right, the hunter fitted an arrow into his bow, stood up quickly, and sent off a sure shot.

Usually the hunter skinned his prize at once. First he removed the hide from one side and cut the flesh from the bones. Then he worked on the other side. Finally he wrapped the meat of the animal in the hide and carried the bundle back to camp.

A successful hunt meant fresh meat for the family for many days. The Apache women roasted the meat over the fire on long sticks or cooked it in a stew. The Apaches liked meat with fat on it. Men often rubbed the fat on their legs because they believed it would make them as strong and as fast as the animal from which it came.

In warm weather, some meat of the day's hunt was usually cut into strips, dried in the sun, and saved for the next several days. Otherwise the meat would spoil in the hot sun.

Young boys learned to hunt small mammals such as prairie dogs, squirrels, and rabbits. These animals also were used as food for the family.

Gathering Plants

Apaches ate a great variety of wild plants. It was the women's job to gather anything that could be eaten. Two plants that grew in great abundance — yucca and mescal — were staples of the Apache diet. In early spring, the women harvested the yucca plant, which sometimes grew six feet tall. It was called the desert candle because it had a large cluster of white flowers at the end of a slender stalk.

In late spring, the women gathered mescal. This plant had large leaves that grew in the shape of a cabbage head. The women often spent many days at a time gathering enough mescal to feed their families for months.

When the stalk of a young yucca plant was roasted, it was very tender and tasted a bit like asparagus. Older plants that might be tough were pounded and steamed to make them edible. Mescal was always steamed. It tasted somewhat like squash.

Steaming plants was no simple task. The women first built a large fire in a deep pit that was filled with stones. When the fire burned down, the embers were brushed aside and the yucca or mescal was piled on the hot stones. The plants were then covered with wet grass and left to steam for much of the day.

8

Some of the steamed food was later dried and stored for the cold season or for times when the family moved to new camps. Dried plants were wrapped in animal skins and stored in baskets. Apache women did not often make or use pottery because it was too heavy to carry as they moved from place to place. Baskets were common because they could be carried easily.

Other plants the Apaches ate were arrowhead, wild onions, and berries such as sumac, strawberries, raspberries, and grapes. Often, berries were pounded into small cakes and dried in the sun. Berry juice was poured over these cakes and, as they dried, a sugary coating formed. This preserved the fruit cakes for a long time without spoiling.

Apaches gathered many kinds of nuts, including the tiny sweet nut of the pinon pine tree. Pinon nuts are still special favorites of Apache children.

When necessary, the Indian families stored their dried food in large pits over the winter months. The women lined the base and walls of a storage pit with smooth stones and added loose brush. Then the baskets of dried food were placed in the pits and covered with more brush. The opening of the pit was closed with large rocks and finally sealed with a layer of mud. There was no danger of strangers stealing the buried food!

Baskets, Burden Carriers, and Cradleboards

Baskets were important to the early Apaches. The Apache woman used the baskets she made to pack the few possessions of the family each time they journeyed to a new home site. Women made their baskets from a variety of different plants, reeds, and herbs that grew on the plains and mountains.

They mainly used yucca leaves, willow reeds, or juniper bark. First they twisted or braided strands of the plants into long sections. Then they coiled the sections to form small circles or big circles, depending upon the size of the basket needed.

Flowers from other plants were used to make dyes for painting the baskets. The rabbit brush plant made a yellow dye and the devil's claw plant produced a brown dye. For shades of red and lavender, the women used the blooms of flowering cactus.

Apache women used a burden carrier for transporting heavy loads. The burden carrier hung across the woman's back and shoulders. The bottom of the carrier extended straight out to form a small shelf. A piece of deerskin was attached to the top of the carrier like a strap. The woman placed the strap over her head and rested it across her forehead.

The Apache mother also carried her baby on her back, using a cradleboard that kept the baby snug and safe while the mother worked or traveled. A mother often hung the cradleboard from the low branch of a tree while she gathered food for her family. The mother was careful to keep her eye on her baby. An Apache mother was very proud and protective of her family. Each baby wore a charm made of feathers or deer's teeth to protect it from danger or evil spirits.

Apache Clothing

Like most other Indian tribes, the Apaches used deer hide to make clothing in the early years. The women prepared the deer hide by first soaking it in water and then stretching and rubbing it to make the material soft.

The Apaches wore simple outfits. In warm weather, the men wore only breech cloths and moccasins. In cold weather, they wore shirts that came almost to the knees. Their moccasins were like boots that reached to the knee or above. The foot of the moccasin was shaped with a tip that turned up at the toes. The height of the mocassins probably protected the wearer from thorny plants, rocks, and snakes. The soles were covered with tough, untreated animal skins.

The women, too, dressed very simply. They wore skirts in warm weather and simple dresses in cold weather. The edges of their dresses were fringed and sometimes decorated with dried porcupine quills. Their moccasins were like those worn by the men.

The Apache men did not wear large feather headdresses like many other Indians of the West. Instead, they wore a simple headband of deer skin wrapped across the forehead. Both men and women wore their thick, straight black hair very long. It was rare to see hair braided or pulled back.

After the Mexican settlers entered the Apache territory, the Apaches began to wear clothing in the style of the whites. Both men and women wore clothes made of colorful cotton.

(Photo courtesy of Arizona Historical Society)

Mojave Apaches about 1886.

The Apache man wore a shirt with long shirttails, like the Mexicans and Americans. Frequently he wore a vest that might have been taken in a raid. He often wore a sash or a gunbelt wrapped around his hips.

Apache women used cloth of the brightest colors possible — orange, scarlet, and blue — to make skirts, blouses, and dresses. Their skirts were full, sometimes made with many yards of cloth.

Although the Apaches adapted the colorful cotton clothes of whites, they never abandoned moccasins. Both males and females continued to wear their traditional, knee-high deerskin footwear.

13

Spirits and Ceremonies

The Apaches believed that everything in nature had special power. They also believed that some animals were possessed of evil spirits or ghosts that must be avoided. Those animals included the bear, owl, and coyote. The crow, however, was sometimes a sign of good luck. If warriors spotted a crow before a raid, they believed they would be victorious.

Above all the minor spirits, both good and evil, was the Great Spirit. According to legend, the Great Spirit sent the Mountain Spirits or Ganhs to the Apaches to show them how to live a good life. The Ganhs instructed the Indians to be kind to one another, to take care of the helpless, and to be fair.

The Ganhs taught the Apaches many ceremonies and chants to overcome dis-

ease and call for blessings from the Great Spirit. The Apaches followed the instructions of the Ganhs for some time, but soon began to ignore their teachings. The Ganhs became disgusted with the behavior of the Apaches and disappeared into the mountains.

In time, the Indians began to impersonate the Ganhs and perform ceremonial dances, often around a bonfire. A sick person usually called upon the Ganhs who would dance all night until dawn to drive away the illness. The dancers would whirl and circle in great frenzy. Many times during the dance the dancers would touch the sick person with a wand. The Indians believed that the illness was absorbed into the wand and blown away with the wind as the dancers moved. The dance of the Ganhs is still performed today at special ceremonies and tourist events.

A Ganh impersonator is easily identified by the unusual towering headdress he wears. The face of the dancer is always covered with a deerskin hood. Stems of plants, tree limbs, or pieces of wood are shaped or carved into decorative patterns and attached to the top of the hood. Some shapes resemble sunbursts and others might look like antlers. Sacred symbols are painted into the patterns. Ganh dancers signal their approach by the clatter of their headdresses.

The Ganh dancer also wears eagle feathers tied to the ends of long streamers wrapped around his arms. In his hand he carries a long pole or sword that is used as a wand or a weapon.

The traditional dance of the Ganhs was performed each year at the coming-of-age ceremony for a young Apache girl. Even today some Apaches conduct this ceremony. The ceremony is a four

day festivity for a maiden between the ages of twelve and fourteen to mark the beginning of womanhood. Today, tourists visiting Indian reservations in New Mexico are often allowed to witness this traditional ceremony.

Many Apache families gather for this event. The adults and young males celebrate at a long distance. A special hut is constructed for the young girl. The hut is called the Big Tepee. It stands twenty-five feet high and is made with four main poles and eight supporting poles. It opens to the east so the girl can celebrate the dawn.

For the first three days, the girl remains inside the tepee and performs many rituals. A special costume of golden buckskin is presented to the girl. One woman serves as the leader of the ceremony. She washes the girl's hair with special plant juices and paints her

Mescalero Apache Crown Dancers.

(Photo courtesy of Arizona Historical Society)

An Apache family.

body with pollen. The woman instructs the young girl on how to be a good wife, a good mother, and a good woman. In the background, old shamans — medicine men — chant ceremonial songs.

During these days, the young girl cannot drink water except through a small reed. She is not allowed to laugh or smile because that might cause wrinkles to appear on her face.

Many believe the young girl has special powers at this time. She is recognized as the symbol of Mother Earth. Sick people hoping to be healed ask the girl to lay her hands on them.

If the young girl behaves well throughout the ceremony, she will have a good and honorable life.

On the last day of the ceremony, a shaman blesses the girl and chants these words:

"The sun . . . has come down to the earth. It has come to give her . . . long life. Its power is good."

There is no similar coming of age ceremony for a young man. However, boys at age twelve are allowed to participate in ceremonial races that last for several days. Both old and young men participate in the races. They do not race to beat others. Instead, they race to return energy to the Life Giver, the Sun. They believe that their combined energies are needed to assist the sun god in spreading life-giving warmth over the earth.

The Ganh dancers also appear at this celebration and chant prayers to ward off evil. One prayer that they chant has these words:

"Beautiful is the Mother Earth. Above her are the white clouds. Under the clouds, the sun is shining. In the warm sunshine, among the green herbs, I walk where sunbeams are dancing."

Apache Tribal Bands

From the mid-1700s to 1848, the Apaches were in frequent conflict, first with the Spanish and then the Mexicans. These whites had moved deep into Apache territory in what is now Arizona, Texas, and New Mexico.

By this time, the Apaches had separated into several bands. They considered themselves related but they took different names and lived in different regions of the Southwest. Three bands lived far from the conflict with the Mexicans. One was the Lipan Apache, living in what is now Texas. Another was the Western Apache, who lived north of what is now Phoenix, Arizona. The third band was the Jicarilla (pronounced Hickor-eea), which lived in the northern part of what is now New Mexico.

Three other bands lived closer to the Mexican settlements. Those bands were the Mimbreno, Mescalero, and the Chiricahua (pronounced Cheer-a-cow-a). It was the Chiricahua who most often engaged in skirmishes with the Mexicans. This band had many subgroups which were very warlike. They earned a reputation for the Chiricahua as the most hated Apaches — hated even by other Apaches.

The Chiricahua bitterly fought the white invaders of their lands. For a long time, they resisted conquest. The history of the Chiricahua is remembered through the stories of their great leaders: Mangas Coloradas, Cochise, and Geronimo, whose name is still a war cry. These men correctly saw the white settlements as invasions of their lands and attempted to save their lands by opposing the U.S. government.

(Photo courtesy of Arizona Historical Society)

Apache scout in the 1880s.

Before 1848, the young nation of the United States had not expanded its control to the Southwest. The only Americans who came in contact with the Apaches were beaver trappers and traders, some of whom were illegally in Mexican territory. At first, the Apaches viewed these early Americans as rather harmless because they were not making permanent settlements at that time.

The Mexicans, on the other hand, were a serious threat to the Apaches. In 1821, the Mexicans gained their independence from the Spanish. They then were eager to conquer the Indians once and for all. One way they succeeded in eliminating many Apaches was by paying generous sums of money to hunters who brought in Apache scalps.

Bounty for Scalps

The Mexican government offered 100 pesos for the scalp of an Apache male, fifty pesos for the scalp of a female, and twenty-five pesos for the scalp of a child. In the 1830s, the peso was equal in value to the American dollar. Bounty hunting for scalps set off brutal raids and massacres of Apaches. Along with the Mexicans, some Americans became scalpers.

One such American was a trader named James Johnson who sold guns, livestock, and foodstuffs to Indians. The Apaches trusted Johnson and did not consider him an enemy. They were wrong. Johnson set a trap to catch an Apache who was among the "most wanted" by the Mexicans.

The Apache's name was Juan José. He had been educated by the Spanish and could read and write the language of the Mexicans. He used this skill to raid military mails and got information about troop movements and shipments of guns. The Mexicans considered him extremely dangerous.

In 1835, trader Johnson lured Juan José and a party of thirty-five Apaches to a meeting along the Gila River. Johnson pretended that he had gifts of blankets, whiskey, and saddles for Juan José and his followers. Instead, Johnson set off an explosion and killed the group. Johnson collected bounty for twenty-five scalps. Other members of the tribe retaliated by destroying Johnson's trading post. Johnson escaped and left the area before they could kill him.

Johnson was just one of hundreds of greedy, evil men who killed Indians for money. Some scalpers are reported to have earned thousands of dollars for their brutal behavior. It was these whites, not Indians, who deserved to be called savages. As whites massacred and scalped Apaches, the Indians struck back. They, in turn, massacred whites — both Mexicans and Americans. Scalping for money had tragic consequences. Relationships between whites and all tribes of Indians of the Southwest were deeply affected.

"Tigers of the Human Species"

Apache Indians had a long history of hostility toward others. General George Crook, who campaigned against them, called them the "tigers of the human species." They were among the fiercest and most feared Indians of the Southwest for more than two hundred years. From the early 1600s to 1886, Apaches terrorized those who invaded their lands. Generation after generation of Apache men developed their skills as raiders and warriors. They viewed raiding as a way of life, filled with adventure as well as great danger.

An Apache youth served a long training period before he could become a warrior. He developed his survival skills by spending many days in the rugged mountains, living only on the food he could find. He had to travel as much as seventy miles a day on foot with very little water. At age seventeen, a youth who could provide for himself could become a warrior.

The night before a raid, everyone gathered around a fire. There the shaman — medicine man — called upon the spirits to protect the warriors. It was believed that the shaman could also predict the future. Sometimes he advised against the raid because he could foresee overwhelming danger.

The shaman painted the bodies of the warriors with ceremonial red and black paint. Then he chanted and beat his drum as each warrior performed a dance while the others watched. The dances were like a rehearsal of the next day, showing the spirits how the warriors expected to twist and turn and dodge

(Photo courtesy of Arizona Historical Society)

Na-huash-i-ta, an Apache medicine man.

the arrows and weapons of the enemies.

In the early years, these warriors used simple but effective weapons: bows and arrows, lances, and clubs made from animal bones. The points of the arrows and lances were made of pieces of flint. The flint — known as an arrowhead — was finely honed and sharpened to a deadly point that could quickly invade its victim.

After extended contact with the Spaniards and Mexicans, most Apaches acquired the white man's weapon — the gun. This was usually a rifle. The first

21

rifles the Indians used were usually stolen. In time, they began to trade for guns or buy them directly from sellers who were acting illegally.

Before the Apaches had horses, they made all their raids on foot. They sometimes traveled for days before reaching their destinations. Then they might have to wait for hours until they could take their victims by surprise. That time usually came before daybreak or when women and children were alone in the enemy's camp.

By the early 1700s, the character of Apache raids changed due to the use of the horse, which the Indians had acquired from the Spanish. The Apaches became excellent riders, but never raised horses. Whenever they needed horses, they stole them or took them in a raid.

The Apache raider was clever, cautious, patient, and swift. He could outwit and outrun most white enemies. He knew how to create fear in whites. Frequently he would wear down whites by tracking his prey for many days before taking action.

Attacks on whites were often in retaliation for brutal attacks on the Apaches. The Indians usually had the advantage of being familiar with the rugged, mountainous lands that were foreign, particularly to early settlers.

A typical attack on whites started as groups of Apaches took positions on high cliffs overlooking a camp or settlement. From time to time, they would show themselves and then vanish. This served to make the whites uneasy. The Indians sent up smoke signals from many spots, and that frightened the whites even more. At night, the Apaches would sit in the darkness near the camp and make sounds like a coyote or hooting owl to further increase the pressure.

Next the Apaches would stage a series of small assaults. Maybe they would come silently out of the darkness to steal horses and mules. Maybe they would sneak into small settlements or camps, taking one or two captives.

If those actions did not drive off the whites, the Apaches staged a major attack. A large group of warriors rode through the area and killed the people. Usually the Apaches did not burn homes because they feared the spirits that might inhabit the people who died in the fire. Apaches were great believers in what we call ghosts.

Mangas Coloradas.

Apache council.

The Great Chiefs

Mangas Coloradas was an important leader who organized and united several Apache bands before 1848. He knew that the Apaches must unite if they were to have any hope of survival against the power and treachery of the whites.

Mangas Coloradas, meaning "Red Sleeves," was the name he was given by whites. Mangas was a Mimbreno Apache, one of the strongest groups of that time. The Chiricahua band supported the Mimbreno after Cochise, their leader, married a daughter of Mangas Coloradas.

"Red Sleeves" was a physical giant. He stood six feet six inches tall, with strength that matched his height. He was a very intelligent man who negotiated with the leaders of the U.S. Army that were assigned to the Southwest after 1848.

The year 1848 is important in the history of the United States. It is the year that the United States signed the Treaty of Guadalupe Hidalgo with Mexico. This treaty expanded the borders of the United States to the Pacific Ocean and the Rio Grande River.

By this treaty, the U.S. also agreed to take responsibility for keeping the Indians of the Southwest, particularly the Apaches, from crossing the new border and raiding Mexicans. The U.S. further agreed to make the Indians return any Mexican captives they might have in their possession.

The president of the United States at the time was James Polk. He was determined to expand the frontiers of the country and so agreed to these unreasonable terms. It became the job of the U.S. Army to enforce these agreements and control the Indians. It was not an easy assignment.

From 1848 to 1853, there were more than 8,000 soldiers stationed at forts in the Southwest — mainly New Mexico and Arizona. This number was two thirds of the entire U.S. Army at the time. Their main task was to control not

only the Apache bands but also the Commanche, Kiowa, Ute, and Navajo tribes in that area.

In the beginning, Mangas Coloradas and the Apaches accepted the presence of the U.S. Army. That changed after several incidents in which Apache men were killed by white miners. Mangas Coloradas trusted the army leaders and believed they would punish those who murdered Apaches. However, the army did not have control over the civilian judges who decided what sentence should be given to the miners. Light sentences given to men who murdered his brethren forced Mangas Coloradas to realize that there was no justice for his people in the white man's court.

By 1851, the possibility for peace between the Apaches and the Americans was totally destroyed. In that year, Mangas Coloradas himself was cruelly beaten by a group of gold miners. A dozen or more miners, many of them drunk, jumped on Mangas, tied him to a tree, and nearly beat him to death with a whip. Finally the miners freed him. Near death, Mangas returned to his camp and vowed to avenge this attack.

For the next ten years, Mangas Coloradas led bands of Apaches — Mimbreno, Chiricahua, and Mescalero — on the warpath against all whites. He told the Apaches to shoot anyone who wears a hat. Only whites wore hats, of course. It quickly became the custom of the Apaches on the warpath to place a hat on the head of each white they killed.

The U.S. Army chased the bands led by Mangas Coloradas for more than ten years. In 1863, in Pinos Altos, New Mexico, soldiers under the command of Brigadier General J.R. West finally trapped Mangas. He was then about seventy years old. A small group of soldiers tricked him by waving a white flag of peace. Mangas and fifteen others were quickly surrounded by more soldiers. Mangas agreed to be taken prisoner if his companions were freed. The soldiers kept their word and freed all but Mangas.

In a few days, Mangas Coloradas lay dead in an army camp. According to Army records, Mangas was shot as he tried to escape. However, it is thought that, instead, he was shot in cold blood by his captors.

One of the tribesmen who rode with Mangas on the day he was caught would continue the battle for another twenty years. The name of that man was Geronimo. He and Cochise, the chief of the Chiricahua, would lead the Apaches in the final bloodbath between the whites and the Apaches.

Cochise was a highly respected leader of his Chiricahua band. He was a tall, strong, intelligent man who communicated easily with the whites.

His personal battle began in 1861. He had been called to a meeting under a flag of truce at Apache Pass with young Lieutenant George Bascom. The two talked in Bascom's army tent while a small group of soldiers and Apaches waited outside. When the meeting was over, it was discovered that a young American boy was missing from his home. Lt. Bascom suspected that the boy was taken captive by Cochise's Apaches.

Cochise denied any knowledge of the boy. Lt. Bascom did not accept his word and ordered his soldiers to hold Cochise and his party hostage. Cochise escaped by cutting a hole in the tent and outrunning his captors. Several of those who were with Cochise were killed, including some close relatives. For the next ten years, Cochise attacked white settlements and U.S. Army wagons. In 1872, he finally signed a peace treaty with the United States. He died in 1874.

Chiricahua Apache scout.

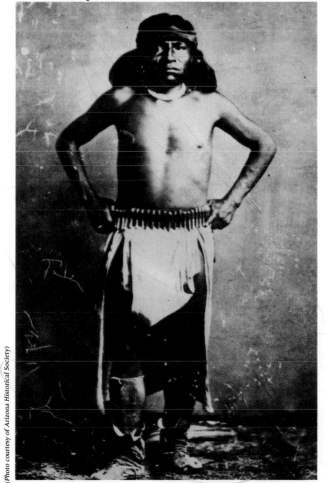

Geronimo, the Last Warrior

In 1852, Mexican soldiers killed Geronimo's wife, three daughters, and mother on the same day. From that time on, Geronimo became increasingly hostile toward whites. As the years passed, he came to be known as the most terrifying Chiricahua, hated even by other Apaches.

By 1874, most of the Apaches had been forced onto reservations. Geronimo was among them. Until that time, he had lived his whole life in the mountains near the Mexican border. He hated living on a reservation where the land was dry and flat. Soon he escaped with a small band of followers. The government called them renegades.

These Apaches made their hideout in the mountains of Mexico. They raided both Mexican and American settlements, killing many people. For ten years, Geronimo and his band were chased by the Army. During those years, the renegades were caught and put on a reservation, but they escaped again and again.

After years of fighting and running, Geronimo surrendered to the U.S. Army on August 25, 1886. With him were twenty-two warriors and fourteen women and children. Today, a pile of rocks marks this historic spot in Skeleton Canyon, Arizona. After Geronimo's surrender, no more Indians of any tribe roamed free in the United States.

Geronimo and his followers spent the rest of their lives as prisoners at Fort Sill, Oklahoma. From time to time, Geronimo was released to be "shown" across the country. He even rode in the inaugural parade for President Theodore Roosevelt in 1905. Geronimo died in 1909. His descendents still reside in Oklahoma.

Apache Indians Today

In 1889, there were about 5,000 Apache Indians living on reservations in very bad conditions. In 1989, there were more than 25,000 Apaches still living on or near reservations. Now the majority have good jobs and lead independent, successful lives.

The six tribal bands of the 1800s have reorganized into three bands: The Chiricahua Apaches, the Eastern Apaches, and the Western Apaches. The smallest band is the Chiricahua Apaches who continue to live mainly in Oklahoma. The Eastern Apaches, who are the descendents of the Mescalero and Jicarilla bands, live in New Mexico. The Western Apaches live in Arizona on three reservations — San Carlos, Tonto, and White Mountain.

Each group is governed by a tribal council that is elected by the people. The council handles matters of education, housing, justice, health, and welfare. They live on reservation lands that are rich in resources, including oil and gas.

Today's Apaches are a success story that is well known among Indian tribes. The White Mountain Apaches (part of the Western band) living in central Arizona are prosperous commercial business people. They developed the Fort Apache Timber Company in 1963 to harvest and sell timber from their vast forestlands. Today the yearly sale of timber brings in more than $14 million dollars. Most people who work for this company are Apaches.

Another successful business operated by this tribal band is the Apache Sunrise Ski Resort. It is one of the most popular ski areas in Arizona. If you visit the resort, most of the workers around you will be Apache Indians. In New Mexico, the Apaches operate the Sierra Blanca Ski Resort, which is also a popular tourist spot.

Arizona today is the home not only of Apaches but also of many other tribes. According to the Bureau of Indian Affairs, there are more than 175,000 Indians of different tribes in Arizona.

At least twenty-six percent of the state's land is owned by Indians, and the Western Apaches control nearly four million acres.

The Mescalero band of the Eastern Apaches have earned a special distinction. They are the first Indians to organize and train as forest fighters. They are known as the famous "red hats."

Today you can find Apache Indians in many occupations. There are cattle ranchers, farmers, miners, teachers, office workers, politicians, truck drivers, and more. Nevertheless, unemployment continues to be a problem for some.

The early history of the Apache Indians is a sad tale of cruel and inhuman treatment. The story of the Apaches today is an inspiring account of a strong, talented, and determined group of people. All Apaches take pride in their accomplishments as Native Americans and citizens of the United States.

Important Dates in Apache History

1589   The Apache Indians are mentioned in the records of Spanish colonizers of the Southwest.

1600s   Wandering bands of Apaches successfully avoid enslavement by Spanish colonizers.

1700s   Apaches, Spaniards, and Mexicans are in continuous conflicts.

1821   Mexico gains independence from Spain and increases attacks against Apaches.

1830s   Mexico offers bounty money for Indian scalps.

1848   United States and Mexico sign the Treaty of Guadalupe Hidalgo which requires the United States to end Apache raids on Mexicans.

1851   Mangas Coloradas, Mimbreno Apache chief, is severely beaten by whites and goes on the warpath for revenge.

1852   Geronimo, a Chiricahua Apache, finds his mother, wife, and children murdered by whites.

1861   Cochise, Chiricahua Apache chief, escapes capture by U.S. Army and goes on warpath to seek revenge for the murder of his relatives.

1863   Mangas Coloradas is killed by U.S. Army.

1871   125 Apache, mostly women and children, are slaughtered in the Camp Grant Massacre in Arizona by members of the Committee for Public Safety.

1872   Cochise signs a treaty with General Howard and agrees to end attacks on whites.

1874   Cochise dies of unknown illness.

1875   Geronimo refuses to live on a reservation and flees to Mexico with a small band of followers.

1876-1886   Geronimo and his band of "renegade" Chiricahua raid Arizona and Mexico.

1886   Geronimo surrenders to the U.S. Army for the final time.

1905   Geronimo rides in the inaugural parade for President Theodore Roosevelt.

1909   Geronimo dies at Fort Sill, Oklahoma.

1963   White Mountain Apaches establish the Fort Apache Timber Company in Arizona.

1989   More than 25,000 Apache Indians live and work on or near reservations in Arizona and New Mexico.

INDEX

*Apache scout
and his violin.*
(Photo courtesy of Arizona Historical Society)